Awakening
the
Spirit Within

Marilyn —
Love and blessings to
dear friend!

Jan Forrest

♡
jan

7/01

Heart To Heart Press

Published by Heart to Heart Press
P.O. Box 215, West Olive, MI 49460
1-800-341-5541
hearttoheart@novagate.com

Editor: Tracy McCasey
Additional Editorial Support: Innernet Affirmations
Cover and Text Art: Laura Dangel-Shaw
Cover Design: Art From the Heart
Composition: Tracy McCasey

ISBN: 0-9663602-9-X

Manufactured in the United States of America

For
Bob,
Casey, Kyle & Taylor

You'll be in my heart
always...

Table of Contents

Introduction

The call to awaken has been sent. The saints and sages who walked this earth in previous centuries beckon us to enter into greater awareness of our lives and how we are living them. They encourage us, by their example, to explore and deepen our relationship with the Divine. The call is still being issued today by visionary men and women who boldly speak of abandoning old ways of being, to live authentic Spirit-filled lives. God Itself whispers (and sometimes shouts) for us to wake up and pay attention to who we are, what we honor and where we are going. To remember our divine nature and capabilities. To align ourselves with a sacred calling.

"The call" comes when we have an awareness, a sense that a veil is lifting to show us ourselves as we are and as we can be. It is a call you have most likely already received, because the act of reading this book, of holding it in your hands, is part of that process. It may be a feeling of dissatisfaction with what is or is not, a desire to know more than what is visible to your eyes. It is what my mentor, Sue Patton Thoele calls, "a deep and holy hunger."

The Divine encourages us to begin the journey inward. This is a most daunting task because for too long we have been taught that the answers we seek are outside of ourselves. With this teacher, that seminar, those books. To believe that all the answers we search for so painstakingly are found inside of us seems a ridiculous notion, for what could we possibly know? We are ordinary people struggling with Universal Truths. Surely, the solutions to our dis-ease are out there somewhere! Nothing could be further from the truth.

Within each of us is a small, divine spark, a glimmer of God Itself. By spending time with and nurturing this glint of divinity, our spirit, we come into greater contact with the Transcendent, deepening our relationship, engaging in communication and communion. Through our inner journey, we come to know ourselves within a sacred framework, and in so doing, experience first-hand the presence of our Source.

In this book, *Awakening the Spirit Within*, I offer reflections on 10 Keys that will unlock the doorway to your spirit, delivering you to the portals of God's own heart. These 10 Keys are ways of seeing and being in the world, forming the core of a daily spiritual practice and lifestyle. They serve as stepping stones on the inner pathway which leads to self-realization, and, if we hold true to where they lead, God-realization.

The Keys are:

Believe	Know we live in a divinely organized universe. Seek to understand its rhythms.
Live in the Present	Slow down, connect with the 'Now.' Fully engage ourselves in conscious living.
Seek Silence	Go within, seek solitude, listen to the voice of Spirit.
Pray	Request divine assistance for the journey.
Give Thanks	Show gratitude for this abundant universe and its blessings.
Find Your Voice	Speak your truth. Honor your inner wisdom.
Open Your Heart	Live from the wide open spaces of your heart where Love resides.
Be Love	Mirror divine Love. Be God's presence in the world.
Trust	Know we are divinely loved and guided.
Surrender	Offer ourselves to Spirit and honor where It leads.

The ponderings I offer you are randomly delivered throughout this text. There is no order or sequence to their presentation. I suggest that whenever you are moved to seek guidance, haphazardly choose a page to peruse, knowing you will be innately guided to the one you need at that exact moment. If you seek deeper insight into one of the 10 Keys specifically, the index at the close of the book can indicate where to find it throughout the text. Allow your inner guidance system to lead you through these musings. It will take you where you need to go.

And so the call has been issued. Will you come forward and discover who you are and who you are not? If you choose to answer the summons, that loud knock on the door of your heart, be prepared to risk all you hold dear. You will leave old life ways behind, embarking on a bold, new journey to awakened living. My prayer is that the words penned here in this little volume will provide sustenance for your journey, food for your soul, and the courage to go the distance. Spirit awaits.

Abundant Blessings,
Jan Forrest

March 2000

There is only one time when it is essential to awaken.
That time is now.

– The Buddha

In an increasingly complex and frustrating world,
we long for Love.
We long to know God intimately.
We seek an all-consuming relationship with the Divine
because we have been thirsty for too long,
and we have sought sustenance from many dry wells.
It is time to drink from the cup of Spirit,
allowing ourselves to become intoxicated by its sweetness,
opening our eyes to limitless beauty
and Love beyond measure.

What a blessing it is to do nothing, to just "Be."
Surrender all thoughts of past events
and future worries to Spirit
and settle into the beauty of the moment.
Delight and savor the sounds, sights, and smells
of wherever you are at this instant.
As you do so, you will sense newfound appreciation
for what it means to be a vibrantly alive human being.

Allow yourself the opportunity to move away

from all the demands of everyday life.

Sequester yourself and rest in the arms of the Divine.

Give yourself permission to be gently held in spiritual silence by

your Higher Power

who knows of your need

to be lovingly embraced and comforted.

A baby cries out when it needs something,

when it is hungry or needs to feel a loving presence.

By crying, an infant lets his or her needs be known.

It is also one of the things we unlearn in adulthood.

When we are lost or lonely we harbor our anger inside of us,

hesitant to cry out, certain we can handle it ourselves.

We grieve in isolation, yet, it need not be so.

There is always One Who Listens.

Spirit is a constant in our lives.

We are never alone.

Our cries do not fall on deaf ears.

Comfort yourself in knowing that the Divine One

is always at hand to dry our tears

and soothe the small, injured child within us all.

As you find yourself enjoying nature,

give thanks for its beauty.

Allow your spirit to soar as you witness its everyday miracles.

Whether you notice a seagull flying high above the ground

or finger the velvety soft petals of a blossoming rose,

allow yourself to be nurtured, fed, and enriched

by our first and forever Mother — the Earth.

Throughout our lives, we are guided and directed by others.

There comes a time

when we must follow our own inner compass.

By listening to your heart

and following its gentle wisdom,

your inner compass will guide you

in the direction of your dreams.

Find your 'true north' and follow where it leads.

Trust that it will take you where you need to go.

As we voyage through life,
we are gifted with companions for the journey.
As our spiritual lives shift and change,
our fellow travelers change as well.
As we learn to live authentic Spirit-filled lives,
we will meet others who are doing the same.
Because we are not intended to travel alone,
the Divine provides us with voyagers who are like us.
It is important for us to keep company with others who
understand spiritual unfolding and who can help us stay on track.
The miraculous part of the process is that rarely
do we have to actively seek out such individuals.
Spirit has an uncanny way of
placing them directly on our path
just when we need them the most.

It is easy to love those who love us —
more difficult to love those who don't.
The challenge is to evolve ourselves to the point
where we see and experience Spirit in all forms.
We never know where God's messengers will be found.
Rumi, the Persian poet and sage counseled us,
"Be grateful for whomever comes,
because each has been sent as a guide from beyond."
The Divine is found in every form,
whether it be a fellow soul traveler with whom
we have instantaneous connection,
the irksome stranger who tests our patience,
or the loved one who is a perpetual thorn in our side.
All are of the One.

In the process of our own awakening,
we cannot compare our growth to anyone else's.
Each of us is growing emotionally, intellectually,
and spiritually at our own pace,
in our own fashion, toward our highest purpose.
Each of us is exactly where we are meant to be right now —
in a growth pattern that is uniquely our own,
on a path that is ours and ours alone.

Wherever we go, God is.

Whatever path we choose,

whatever twists and turns we encounter,

the Divine Presence can be felt if we are but aware.

We are never alone.

Our personal connection to Spirit is amazingly evident, alarmingly

simple, if we can only attune ourselves to it.

Turn off your thoughts

and relish the beautiful physicality of this planet,

so alive with color and wondrous sights

which delight the senses.

A world which allows itself to just "BE"

for it can do nothing else.

Can we follow the most perfect example of Mother Earth

and simply BE in and of this world,

day by day, moment by moment as she does?

She just IS and we can be, too.

It is alright to be still.

It is good to rest.

Even slumber can restore us to our vibrant selves.

Close your eyes.

Shut out the noise and commotion of everyday existence.

Engage in sacred rest,

a time of nurturing your weary inner spaces.

Ernest Holmes, author of *Science of Mind*, wrote,
"Our prayer is answered before it is uttered."
This can be a tremendous source of comfort to us,
knowing that every unspoken thought and intention
has already been heard by divine ears.
Instead of stumbling and struggling,
we can move confidently forward, secure in the knowledge
that even if our words fail us,
God has heard the murmurings of our heart.

Why do we want to express gratitude for our blessings?

Because the Laws of the Universe tell us

that the more grateful we are,

the more abundance we receive.

When we offer prayers of thanks for all that has been given us,

we complete the cycle of giving.

We give thanks and appreciation for what we received,

demonstrating the law of reciprocity,

an energetic force within the universe that works in circles.

God gives. We give back.

The circle is complete and ready to begin again.

Like the birds, each one of us has a special song to sing.

A song that is ours and ours alone.

A rendition which tells the world of our presence,

our purpose, and goes on to celebrate our existence.

It begins with recognizing and honoring your own voice.

There is only one you.

There is only one individual in this universe

who can do what you can do,

accomplish what you can accomplish.

When we see ourselves for who we truly are,

applauding our gifts and talents and offering them to the world

as our 'gift of song,' we have arrived.

What is your unique song

that you can contribute to the adagio of life?

As you prepare yourself for the deeper recesses
of your own awakening,
be aware of the relationships that begin
to form at this juncture of your soul growth.
They are here to sustain you,
assist you, and walk by your side
as you move through any intensity
you may encounter on the journey
to your highest self.

As our inner journey deepens,

our hearts expand with love.

Because we have opened our hearts to God,

and as long as we keep this heart connection fluid and open,

we become conduits for others

to experience Divine Love as well.

This outpouring of heavenly love

that we have received

can be passed on to everyone we meet.

You will come into fruition in your own season.

Just as the daffodils of spring unfold in accordance

with Divine Order, so must we.

Often, we find this process to be frustratingly slow,

but it is right and true to the higher purpose

to which we have been called.

Like the daffodils,

let us be gentle with ourselves

as we strain to reach out and up,

raising our own beautiful crowns to the celestial light.

If we could envision our lives like the ocean,

we would see that it is the Divine who provides the waves.

Those circumstances and events which come our way

every single day are the Universe's way of providing lessons for us

to grow and become who we are meant to be.

We never know whether they will be

gentle rollers or pounding surf.

We must be prepared to receive whatever we are given.

If we put our faith

in the workings of the Universe,

we would ride the waves of spiritual growth

and more easily surf through the waters of life.

Why do we want to strive to spend more time

in the present moment?

Because as we do, our minds stop racing.

We are at peace.

Everyday stresses are gone.

We experience a deeper connection to life,

its daily events, joys, and sorrows.

In the present moment we feel vibrantly alive.

Seedlings rest in the moist soil of Mother Earth's womb
before they grow to fruition.
Periods of stillness enliven our spirit,
enabling us to become more fully
who we are meant to be.

As we hike through the hilly terrain of life,

we may stumble along the path,

striking our feet

against deeply embedded roots

or immovable boulders.

Unsure of how to carry on, we cry out in prayer.

We beg Source for assistance,

to reveal a way in which we can maneuver

around these obstacles.

Struggling for the correct words,

we implore the Divine to do our work for us,

sever the roots, move the boulders, and ease our burden.

Trust that your prayers will be answered.

Spirit may not provide what you ask for,

but will give you what you need to move forward.

Even in negativity, abundance is present.

Every less than desirable situation,

heartbreak or loss is accompanied by a lesson.

Negative experiences may be a universal call

to wake up or take notice.

When we look for the greater lesson to be learned,

we can see much abundance,

though at first glance it may seem to not be so.

Ask yourself, "What lesson am I supposed to learn here?"

Seek the gift in each situation.

Buried treasure may lie underneath the compost of life.

Seek to unearth the blessings within.

It is not an easy task being a person of vision.

Whenever we speak our truth,

we run the risk of criticism and public denouncement.

Others may not share our world view.

By raising our voices,

communing with like minds

to shape a world of peace, love, and beauty,

we honor ourselves.

In doing so, we also give others permission to do the same.

As we open our hearts while
learning to express our authenticity to the world,
we attract others of like energy who enhance our journey.
Openness makes us more vulnerable,
but telling our own truth
gives others permission to do the same.
Living in an authentic, heart-wide-open manner
draws similar people to us
and increases our own support system.
The result is a newfound sense of strength all around.
Just as a vine sends out strong tendrils as it grows,
this expansion supports its own growth
as well as those whom it entwines.

The term 'unconditional love' is more
than a current metaphysical buzz word,
more than the sum of its syllables.
The mission of enlightened beings
is to immerse ourselves in the divinity of God,
and to see Him/Her
in the eyes of every human being we encounter.
As we deepen our personal awareness of the Divine,
we take on more and more spirit-filled characteristics.
Instead of speaking of love, we become love.
We embody love in every thought and action.
What we once thought of as God,
we can now see in the faces of others.

Each one of us awakens
and grows into our spiritual nature
at our own rate.
For some, it will take many seasons
to realize our highest potential
and come into our own fullness.
This is a journey that cannot be rushed, judged, or compared.
Allow yourself to unfold and mature as Spirit intended.
Put your lamentations and worries aside.
Trust in the well-timed beauty of your own growth.

As humans, we long to control
and be in charge of our lives.
Instead, could we intuit and sense through inward reflection how
to best deal with each peak and valley
presented to us on the journey?
How do we best balance ourselves
to receive the next onslaught gracefully?
With Spirit at the helm,
we begin to sense how and when
to climb, to rest, to persevere or to let go.
If we can lessen our grip,
give up some modicum of control
and put the expedition in Spirit's hands,
we just might be amazed at the outcome.

Living in the present takes full effort and concentration.
When we practice living in the 'now,'
we realize each moment is special.
We will never experience this exact circumstance
in this way again.
We will never see these sights, hear these words,
feel these emotions in the same way ever again.
Concentrate on savoring and enjoying the moment at hand
so it is not a lost jewel, but a valued treasure.

Feel the calm which enters you when in a place of great beauty.

Breathe it in.

This is God's breath mingling with yours

which centers and energizes you.

Have you ever given thanks for unanswered prayers?

Jean Ingelow wrote, "I have lived to thank God

that all my prayers have not been answered."

In times of desperation, we implore Spirit to come to our aid,

beseeching intervention, healing, deliverance.

We beg for the relationship, the job, more money, the cure,

confident that we alone know what is best for us.

We can relinquish the need to be in control of our prayers, praying

instead for the Divine One to guide us toward

our greatest good, the highest outcome for all involved.

In asking for specific results, we deny ourselves access

to a deeper wellspring of wisdom found in the Divine Mind.

Pray for guidance.

Let God handle the details.

"The wailing of broken hearts is the doorway to God,"
so said the poet, Rumi.
God certainly hears our cries and acknowledges our pain.
Yet, even as we cry out to God,
we open ourselves to a greater love
than the one we may be mourning.
Through this divine connection, through tears to heaven,
we may experience for the first time
what it feels like to know cosmic comfort and unconditional love.

Each one of us, if given the opportunity,

could deliver a litany of personal injustices, betrayals, and losses.

Cruel blows of fate like cancer, miscarriage, divorce or joblessness

find their way into our lives.

When they visit, we mourn their arrival

and work through their agonies.

Yet, Providence gives us the fortitude

to deal with their blows and, as a result,

shape ourselves into finer people.

This is precisely how life works.

With bad, comes good. With light, comes dark.

With tears come laughter. With sorrow, comes joy.

With pain comes healing.

We cannot have one without the other.

The results of trauma may bring us blessings in disguise.

In this new millennium,

each of us is beckoned

by those who have gone before us

to come out from the shadows.

It is time to compose our own song,

raise our voices and sing exuberantly

with great clarity of our vision for a new day.

We can choose to enter the millennium with pessimism

or we can enter with vision,

hopes, and dreams of the highest caliber.

The choice is ours.

Friends are emissaries of the Divine.

They hold our hands on this earthly plane as God's

representatives in the physical world.

Their hearts hold ours

in times of travail, through joys and sorrows.

Divine presence can most certainly be felt

in the hands and heart of another.

It is through our personal relationships
that we learn the most about ourselves —
who we are, what we value, what we hold dear.
Our relationships also teach us about our own frailties.
our insecurities, and the wounds of our past.
The partnerships that are the most challenging
are indeed the most precious,
because they will teach us more about ourselves
than we ever dreamed possible.

Trust in the Divine, as an active presence in our life, enables us to
move through the seasons of our soul growth
with a deep sense of security.
Such confidence allows us to advance freely,
maneuvering through the wind gusts of life.
The leaves on trees are firmly rooted to their Source,
yet remain free to move, twist, and turn as they choose.
If leaves can find security and freedom
within the same Source, so can we.

Fear paralyzes us.

It stops us in our tracks, preventing us from moving

in the direction of our soul's purpose.

When we give in to our fear, allow it to hold us hostage,

we become inmates in a prison of our own creation.

By asking ourselves what we are afraid of

and acknowledging its hold on us,

we intuit which keys will unlock the door

of our self-imposed stockade.

By gently easing the key into the locked portals of our heart and

surrendering our fear to the Most High,

we can move into the healing light of day.

Each and every day can be a new beginning.

The magic of a 24-hour day lies in the fact

that when it comes to an end, there can be closure.

Conflicts resolved.

Resentments put aside.

Fears surrendered.

With the dawn of a new day

comes the opportunity to begin again.

Just as the sun rises each day

creating a unique and breathtaking panorama,

so can we paint a fresh and brilliant day for ourselves.

The present moment is truly a gift — a gift that we can leave
unopened and unenjoyed or one which we can joyously unwrap and
savor its beauty and meaning.

The choice is ours.

As we learn to take one day at a time,

to revel in its sweetness and, yes,

to fully experience the sorrows as well,

we move to a place of balance and wholeness in our lives.

As we heighten our awareness

of the uniqueness of each moment,

we slow the pace of our life.

Golden moments become golden hours,

great gifts from a generous and loving Universe.

When was the last time you gave yourself permission
to be alone, to revel in the quiet and peacefulness of solitude?
Being alone with ourselves
provides us the opportunity to slow our outer world,
to get in touch with our inner world.
As we breathe in the silence,
we allow our body to rest,
our mind to become calm
and our spirit to reconnect with the world around us.

The Catholic mystic, Meister Eckhart wrote,

"If the only prayer you ever offer is

'Thank You,' that will suffice."

So often our prayers are supplications.

We ask Spirit for things, people, opportunities.

Our needs naturally bring us to the act of prayer.

Yet, prayers of gratitude, of thankfulness, are important acts

which deepen the connection between ourselves and Spirit.

To offer a heartfelt, "Thank You, God!"

delivers us to the realm of unseen abundance.

We view life as blessed and fruitful instead of scarce;

we begin to live from a place of fullness in our lives.

We are and have enough.

It is difficult to see the good in any tragic situation.

Our unceasing cries of "Why?" ring out in the night.

We can intellectualize why, we can guess and offer an answer,

but it is only a feeble attempt

to assuage the pain of our broken hearts.

And yet, in the greater scheme of things,

such tragic events can provide 'blessings in disguise.'

It is the result of such incidents, whether they be global disasters

or personal devastation, which often surprise us

with bounteous blessings beyond our wildest imaginings.

As we experience these events, we develop a greater awareness of

our personal courage and strength, of our capacity

to show love, compassion, and support to others.

Such trials do indeed show us

what we are made of and the goodness within.

Inside each one of us are dark recesses,
corners of our psyche that deserve to be enlightened.
As we journey inward, seeking the Light,
we are hesitant to explore the darkness within.
Our own inner light,
our qualities of goodness, generosity, and love
act as a spiritual flashlight,
allowing us to focus its high-beamed intensity
on the dark nooks and crannies inside —
little corners where selfishness, prejudice, or envy may reside —
all the dark qualities that we deny.
Secrets revealed in the dark bring light to a new way of being.
Be not afraid of your shadows.
They are but deep pools of murky thought
waiting to be illuminated and transformed into brilliant wisdom.

Allow Spirit to mend the cracks of your heart.
The Master Mender knows how to weave threads of joy and
happiness throughout the fabric of your being,
if you will but let it be so.

As we journey inward,

we may be urged to examine the true nature

of our intimate relationships.

Seldom do they resemble the photos on cards

depicting lovers passionately entwined

in front of a glorious ocean sunset.

In real life, our relationships are full of ups and downs,

periods of challenge balanced with periods of great joy.

If anything, these periods are our greatest teachers.

Our personal journey to authentic Spirit-filled living is validated

not by being alone, but in relationship with others.

Learning how to love, teaches us how to live.

As the gardeners of our lives,

we can take all the steps necessary

to ensure the crop of an abundant existence.

We can prepare ourselves, nurture ourselves, and

give ourselves what we need to grow and blossom,

but that is where the labor ends.

We can only do so much.

We must turn the results of our labors over to the Universe.

We must wait and see what grows.

Patience is in order

as we surrender to the will of the Master Gardener.

Everything grows in its own season,

in perfect timing with the cosmic plan

which has been laid out for us.

Fear is a thief.

It will rob you of precious energy, focus,

and attention to your dreams.

Like a prowler who comes in the night,

stalking the hallways of your heart,

it will steal your most valuable attributes — self assurance,

endurance, strength, and inner knowing — if you allow it to do so.

Remember, fear is only a resting place,

a brief moment to remind you of your humanity and fallibility.

Do not rest with it long.

Instead, recall your divinity

and keep moving in the direction of your heart's urging.

We get endless second chances in this lifetime on earth.

Every day we have the opportunity to forgive,

to let go, and move on.

We can give up the bad habit, the unfulfilling job,

the loveless relationship,

and create the life we dream of and deserve.

As the sun rises, bringing the dawn of a new day,

celebrate and give thanks

for the blessing of second chances.

Imagine that you are seeing, hearing, tasting,

touching, smelling —

all for the very first time.

When you venture out into Mother Nature,

breathe in the beauty of these glorious days.

Behold the colors of the Master Painter's handiwork.

Take a mental photograph and log it in as a forever memory

to be called upon when you need sustenance.

Savor the moment.

Within each of us are the answers to our deepest questions.

Silence is the only way to access those answers.

We have been conditioned to believe that the answers

to life's dilemmas are "out there somewhere."

Nothing could be more untrue.

The deepest wisdom lies within.

Within silence are more answers and insights

than we ever dreamed possible.

"Ask and it shall be given to you."

Many religious traditions teach this belief about prayer.

It illustrates the assumption that our Higher Power

is ever present and receptive to our needs and desires.

The power of prayer is in the asking.

In petitioning Spirit for assistance,

we open ourselves to greater goodness.

In surrendering control and admitting we need the Divine

to guide us, heal us, sustain us,

we expand our own capabilities by receiving the gifts of Spirit.

The sheer magnitude of beauty found on this fair planet

is testament alone to the power of Spirit.

From a loving Source, we have been gifted a home

of unparalleled loveliness and brilliance.

From sun-drenched beaches

to snow-capped mountains,

we can pause and give thanks

for the generosity of One who loves us enough

to surround us with sacred handiwork

each and every day.

Heed the still, small voice within

which speaks to you at the most unexpected times.

It is Inner Wisdom calling your name.

This innate sense of knowing has been ours from birth,

yet as we grow into logical, rational adults,

we may have negated its vocalizations.

We dismiss it as inner nonsense,

certain that the mind is the truest source of insight.

Bypass the urge to squelch the sweet sounds of Spirit

bubbling through your core of resistance.

Pay attention.

These words of Inner Wisdom matter.

Each of us has experienced a broken heart
many, many times.
Our hearts break due to disappointment, betrayal, loss.
As we suffer heartbreak, our hearts shatter wide open,
bleed, and experience immeasurable pain.
As a survival mechanism, we quickly try to repair the cracks,
to cement them shut to stop the hurt.
However, it is only through the broken heart
that we learn to love.
It is specifically through these wide open crevices
that we let love come in and allow love to go out.
If the cracks have been mended shut, we cannot do either.

The attitudes and behaviors that we scorn in others
will be the ones that will offer us
the grandest personal and spiritual growth.
When we witness things like rudeness,
selfishness, arrogance, insensitivity, or callousness
we can remind ourselves to exhibit its opposite.
When you see someone act in this fashion,
consciously choose not to walk that path.
Choose the higher road,
the one characterized by compassion and forgiveness.
You may be surprised how your choice
of "the road less traveled"
may be the one they choose to walk in the future.
Be your own best example.

As creative beings, we are accustomed
to charting the days of our lives.
In the true spirit of co-creation,
we only need do our part of the work.
God does the rest.
As we become more cognizant of the role we can play
in this earthly sphere, as we move towards self-realization,
we begin to understand how much of our life
is indeed out of our hands.
By trusting in Source and the job It will do for us,
we become active partners in co-creating
a brilliant life for ourselves.

When life's events carry us
to the point of confusion or frustration,
we may be well served to take a deep breath
and walk away.
Moving away from a situation,
even for a few moments,
can release us from its emotional hold.
Only then can we see the situation clearly.
Ask Spirit to provide you with guidance and lucidity
so you might see the higher purpose of this drama.

The tears we shed that often accompany the broken heart

can indeed take us to heaven into the arms of Spirit.

While sitting in the lap of the Universe,

we receive comfort and courage for the journey.

We receive assurance that our broken heart,

in time,

will heal.

The journey to awakening can sometimes feel like a lonely one.
The story of *The Ugly Duckling*, by Hans Christian Anderson,
comes to mind to illustrate this impression.
We may feel like a swan trapped inside a duckling's body,
surrounded by a community that does not understand us.
We are changing — we are becoming swans,
but no one else seems to recognize it.
Feelings of not fitting in, not belonging
to this earthly existence, flow through our veins.
Because Spirit is generous and knows better than we do what we
require to grow and thrive, we are often gifted
with new companions for the journey.
New companions come to us in the form of teachers, gurus,
masters, angels, and most importantly, friends, who comfort us
and assure us that no one makes the journey alone.

It is healthy to slow down,

to give ourselves much deserved rest and relaxation.

Our bodies are not intended, nor constructed for

such fast-paced living as we are experiencing today.

As passengers on the train of life,

we often move at breakneck speeds.

When we slow down or stop this hasty pace,

we immediately feel better – our bodies and minds tell us so.

We feel inner and outer peace.

Our breath is calm and even.

We feel as if we have found our center once again.

Slowing down brings us home to ourselves.

Moments of solitude enable us to reconnect with our inner self,
to gain needed insights or to connect with Spirit.
These things cannot be achieved without silence.
Our thoughts must slow enough to make room
for new and insightful ones to come forward.

Prayer is an outpouring of the substance of our souls.

As we petition Source,

our words flow,

pouring out our heart's desire,

the water of our being.

We empty our vessel and in so doing,

allow the Divine to fill it again with sweet nectar

to quench our spiritual thirst.

If every time
we felt the beat of our heart
we were reminded to utter,
"Thank You,"
what an abundant life we would have!

God speaks through the whisperings of the heart.

Divine wisdom flows to us through our heart center.

We can feel (intuit) when it is right and true for us.

The voice we hear comes in small murmurings,

gently urging us to move this way or that.

Take this path or follow that lead.

This is the voice of Spirit reaching out

to join with ours in co-creation.

The heart broken wide open,

left to heal with crackles of light peeking through,

allows love to flow in and out to our fellow travelers.

These cracks also serve as direct conduits to the Divine and

enable us to move forward on our spiritual path.

As much as we would like to patch the holes in our broken hearts,

move quickly beyond the suffering and forget it ever happened,

the greatest lessons are learned through experience.

When the pain is too great to bear or our agony

veils the clarity that will eventually come from a heart broken open,

we can take comfort from the 12th-century Persian poet, Rumi,

who wrote, "Keep looking at the bandaged place."

That is where the light enters you."

The beauty of a relationship comes in allowing it to blossom.
Just like a flower,
an intimate partnership does not bloom over night.
It takes time to coax its inherent beauty
to come forth and be seen.
In the initial stages of love, we feel giddy with excitement
at its newness and passion. Over time, as the thorns of life begin
to creep to the surface, we may become less enamored
with our garden variety, certain that it is deeply flawed,
and will never glow with brilliance again.
We can learn from the example of the Master Gardener
who never gives up on our love, even though we may be less than
apt pupils. The cosmic qualities of patience, perseverance,
nurturance, encouragement, and support can allow the bloom of
love to flourish once more.

Our soul growth has its own seasons.
Just as the natural world moves to a higher rhythm,
a manifest pattern year after year, so do we.
Each one of us, as we journey to a higher level of being,
will go through seasons of our own soul growth.
We will have springs, summers, falls and winters,
times of fallow and abundance, darkness and light.
When flowed with and experienced naturally,
without resistance, these seasons will take us
to the next destination on our inner voyage.

The season of autumn urges us
to begin the process of self-analysis, to examine our 'true colors.'
Like the aspen leaf, struggling to hang on to its branch of origin,
we can hold on with great resolve,
refusing to give in to the change that beckons.
The leaf doesn't consciously know it is time to let go,
and yet, eventually it does.
As humans, cognizant of our own process,
we sense it may be time to move on,
to let go of what no longer works for us.
Change is inevitable, but letting go is difficult.
Like the leaves, it is up to each of us to let go,
allowing Spirit to gently guide us
to the next phase of our journey.

When we begin to believe

that the universe is a friendly and supportive place,

one which acknowledges that each individual is special, deserving of

abundance and an excellent quality of life,

then we will find our lives changing for the better.

If we believe in the magic of life,

where miracles are found in everyday living,

we align ourselves with positive intent, thoughts, and actions.

In doing so, we can expect the best to come to us.

Slowing down, taking time off, resting, rejuvenating ourselves helps

us to see things more clearly.

With busyness ruling our days,

if often feels like we are living in a fog.

When we make the decision to rest,

we feel our mental fog dissipate.

The veil lifts and we see ourselves, our situation,

for the first time.

When our lives race out of control,

body and mind struggling to keep up,

there is no way we can think clearly.

A slower pace of life can bring newfound clarity

and peace of mind.

It is not an easy task to still the mindless chatter

of our thoughts.

And yet, we must do so

if we are to really hear the gentle whispers of Spirit.

Like the wind, the Divine Voice murmurs ever so softly

into the recesses of our heart.

Such whispers are sweet and one must quiet to hear them.

Be prepared to listen intently.

Seek solitude and prepare your soul

that you may be lovingly guided by the whisperings of Spirit.

It is important for each of us to 'speak our truth' —
to live an authentic life, to give voice to the issues
that need to be addressed
so that each one of us may move forward
and become the person Spirit intends us to be.
Is it possible to honor our own processes
and still be "nice" to others?
In our day-to-day encounters, let us put our egos aside,
our need to be brutally honest,
and dwell for a few moments on the receiver
and the impact our message might have.
Let us seek a more comprehensive picture of truth telling.
Let us search our hearts to find the best, most considerate way
to 'speak our truth,' balancing honesty with compassion.

The open heart is a forgiving heart.
It does not shut its portals in anger and resentment.
It allows other people the opportunity to make mistakes,
embraces them in their wrong doing
and releases them to grow from their experience.
Such forgiveness creates freedom for all involved.

Can you look at another with Jesus' or Buddha's eyes?
Can we see the Divine Spark in each person who comes into our
life? Can we offer them unconditional love and forgiveness as our
Higher Power does for us? This may be one of the most difficult
lessons on the spiritual voyage because it requires us
to cast off our human vestiges of judgment
and expectations of perfection.
Spirit entreats us instead to cloak ourselves
with celestial garments of acceptance and love,
to strive to see the world and our fellow travelers
with sacred vision.

In observing the well-timed cycles found in nature,
we come to the all important realization
that the seasons are something to follow.
Rachel Carson wrote, "There is something infinitely healing
in the repeated refrains of nature – the assurance that dawn
comes after night, and spring after winter."
The spiritual journey follows the same principles.
Celestial light emerges after a dark night of the soul.
Blessings and abundant harvest result
from toiling laboriously in our spiritual fields.
Trust in the sacred cycles
inherent in the natural world of which we are a part.
By cooperating with the seasons of our own soul growth
we can reap their wisdom and illuminate ourselves.

As the inward journey continues,
it is inevitable that we have moments of intense pain
as if we are being laid open to bake
in a relentless, burning hot sun.
It is only through such decimation,
such roasting, that we leave behind
old ways that caused discomfort,
were inauthentic, deceitful, and dishonest.
Love (love of God) strips away all of our pretenses and leaves us
standing naked at the doorway to God's heart.
One cannot move into the highest stages of human and spiritual
growth without the old self being destroyed.
It takes tremendous courage to surrender oneself to the charring
flames of Divine Love.

The spider weaves his web with glistening silver threads.

Each pathway delicately, but assuredly, leads into the next,

a perfect connection.

There is a master plan

but it is difficult to see

as one is actually doing the weaving.

His innate wisdom takes him where he needs to go.

Like the spider, we can follow the silken threads.

In time, there will be a woven masterpiece,

strong and sparkling in the noonday sun.

Give yourself the gift of "unplugging."

You cannot imagine the riches that may come to you or

what magic may be woven into the fabric of your days

until you take the time

to slow down, stop, and surrender to life.

Everyone needs an oasis in the desert of life.

Your personal oasis is waiting for you.

When you find it, drink deeply of its cooling waters.

Relax in the shade of its sheltering palms.

Be satisfied.

Be well.

Spend a few moments in silence each day

to savor the wisdom that falls between syllables.

Let our own tongues remain silent so God's may speak.

In choosing thoughts, feelings, and actions,

we have two sources to operate from — love or fear.

In any situation, we can ask ourselves, "Am I feeling this way,

speaking and acting from a place of love or fear?"

By simply stepping back, releasing ourselves briefly

from the emotional charge of the moment,

we can better assess our motivation.

A deep breath can bring insight

and restore the connection to our heart center,

which always operates from love with Spirit.

The only real choice is Love.

Love is the key.

Every relationship has a holy purpose.
Each encounter, each intimate union
provides our soul with an opportunity to grow.
Through our interactions with others,
we are gifted with the chance of transforming ourselves
into the highest self we can be.
The Universe partners us with those individuals
with whom soul healing may occur.
Discover what it is you are to learn from this person
and they, in return, from you.
As we seek the deeper meaning in our relationships,
we become more cognizant of the plan Spirit has for us.

Relish the seasons of your own growth as they come to you.

Fortify yourself with the predictability of their presence.

Know that you are exactly where you need to be

at this stage of your journey.

Surrender yourself fully

to the sweet lessons they will bring you.

There is no point in resisting.

With the dawn of a new millennium,

the call is issued to surrender to Love.

Now is the perfect moment to relinquish

our pain, our ego, our suffering

and lay it on the altar of Divine Compassion.

Say, "Nay!" to the old, "Yes!" to the new.

Leave your fear behind you

like a tattered robe that no longer fits.

Instead, don a fresh garment of celestial brightness

for the new life you are destined to live

as a Divine Child of the third millennium.

The Divine One knows the bigger picture,

the grand scheme of your life,

where you are headed,

where you are destined to be.

Allow Spirit to lead you there.

In stillness, we become attuned

to the crystal clear urgings of Spirit.

The silence that dominates the gap between thoughts and words

forms a pool into which drop-like pearls of divine wisdom

can be caught and absorbed.

Within these pearls of wisdom,

God indicates to us the much needed guidance we are seeking.

It is only in pristine silence

that these sweet droplets can be heard.

As spiritual beings with an earthly home,

Spirit invites us to be Its presence in the world.

To be a walking, talking, breathing mirror of the Holy One.

In nature's handiwork, we witness divine inspiration.

We are a part of Creation,

so why would we be omitted from this delight?

Just as birds and trees reflect the Source, so do we.

The kindness, compassion, and joy we share with others mirrors

the Divine inspiration behind them.

We can be God's love in the world.

Everything we need to know for life is right here.

All the divine revelations we may travel far and wide to seek

are right here, just outside the window.

The wisdom of the ages

lies in the sage advice offered by nature.

All the heavenly wisdom we need can be found

in the bounty of God's great universe.

Open your eyes, ears, and heart.

Observe.

Immerse yourself in the beauty that surrounds you.

Listen and it will teach you.

In a world bound up in confusion, despair, global suffering,

and disaster, we long for the Divine Embrace.

To know God intimately and, if possible,

to leave the absurdity of this mundane world behind,

even for a moment.

To dance in the arms of Spirit

and rest in them when the dance is done.

It is not enough to sit and worship.

There is a longing to feel God,

to immerse oneself in eternal Love.

This is the mystical path of awakening.

Look at the beauty around you.

The God-given loveliness of birds, flowers, and trees.

Savor it and take it in to the deepest part of your being.

Spirit lives there.

Observe the movements of a river.

It follows a divine directive to flow out from itself.

At times, gently gurgling over pebble-strewn beds.

Other times, roaring, cascading over tumultuous peaks.

Such is the life of a river.

It does not have the foresight to know where it flows,

only that it *is*.

The river trusts its Source from whence it comes.

It trusts that it will empty itself into another vast body

which will embrace its droplets, absorbing them into eternal bliss.

We, too, can flow from Source,

ever faithful that our journey will take us to

our ultimate destination — God awareness.

Synchronicities are God's way of getting our attention.

When an extraordinary chain of events occurs,

we sit up and take notice.

The Divine beckons us to pay close attention,

to look, see, and listen deeply

for the rhythms and meanings

of the silken threads which are being woven for us.

If we can put aside our hesitations and tendency to dismiss such

sacred weavings as coincidence,

we will witness the interconnectedness of all things,

the Divine Will at work in the world.

By following the silken threads of holy guidance, synchronicities,

we move to the next step on our personal pilgrimage.

If we could only behold the bigger picture of our lives,
imagine what inner peace we would find.
What confidence we would have to boldly move forth in the
direction of our dreams, if we could gaze down from above
and witness the dance of life.
What if we could see our lives through heaven's eyes?
Could we observe, as Spirit does,
the twists and turns of our days, and
see greater patterns emerging or lessons repeating themselves?
Since this capability is not fully ours,
trust is in order.
Trust that you will be delivered safely
to the shore of self and God-realization.

We get caught up in the little details of life.

Surrender them to Spirit

and see what few morsels of worry remain,

insignificant crumbs that they are.

We are here at this exact juncture of our life for a reason.

There is no other place we are supposed to be.

The people in our life are here to teach us.

The experience of our days is laden with wisdom

to be gleaned and cultivated.

Even negative situations

will offer profound guidance for your own development.

There is divine purpose in the fabric of your days.

When we have mastered what we need to learn

from people and situations, we will move on.

"All I have seen teaches me to trust the Creator for
all I have not seen," penned Ralph Waldo Emerson.
In the exquisite beauty of this universe,
how can we not see God's handiwork as proof of a divine plan?
In the delightful order of the seasons and cycles of nature,
how can we imagine that such majesty
was a series of random acts, haphazardly created?
The vast capabilities of mankind alone gives testament
to a scope of creative effort that boggles the mind.
The presence of mankind and nature
bear witness to a grandiose plan of epic proportions
of which we are a key part.
Trust the wisdom inherent in the blueprint of our lives.

There are times in our lives when we may feel a sense of
nothingness, times when we feel small or powerless.
We must keep in mind that these feelings
are a phase of our growth.
Observe the incandescent moon,
which journeys through the night sky with its own period of
invisibility, yet moves into luminescence in its own time.
Just as the moon travels through
predictable phases of fullness, so will we.
The tender outline of who we are
and who we will become
is indelibly sketched out for us by the Master Painter.
Like the moon, fullness will be ours.
With divine timing, we too will radiate light
and become the bright orb we are intended to be.

Imagine God as the world conductor of life's symphony.

Through wisdom, Spirit pulls together

the sounds, sights, people, and opportunities

to create the perfect performance.

Because we have a little bit of musical experience,

we are certain we can conduct as well as God.

In actuality, we have not attained maestro status,

and it may serve us better to take a chair,

play our instrument of choice,

and follow the lead of the Master Conductor,

who knows how to elicit a virtuoso performance

from each of us.

One thing we all avoid is pain.

Yet, if we learn from the saints and sages,

we understand that pain is often central

to the spiritual pilgrimage.

Pain from wounds to our body, mind, or spirit

is followed by healing and a deeper awareness.

Our wounds and the lessons learned from their infliction

have created who we are today.

We are who we are because of the trials of fire

we have walked through.

Who are we to decide which pains we should or should not endure?

May our eyes be open to any pain we might suffer

so that we may bear witness to the Divine plan within —

the plan for our greatest growth and highest good.

Is it possible to fully know and experience God firsthand?

If so, how do we come to this place?

One cannot intellectualize the process, though we try to.

We have studied, analyzed, dissected this mystical experience

only to emerge with a handful of meaningless syllables.

One has to experience it to know it to be true.

Spirit entreats us to risk all and

lose ourselves in the arms of God.

In doing so, we make the great leap of faith,

leaving rational thinking behind.

It is the call to fall in love with God, to hold nothing back and to

dive headfirst into the cosmic ocean of Divine bliss,

all the while knowing

that we will be buoyed and rescued by Love itself,

scooped up and warmly nested in the arms of God.

Index

The 10 Keys for Living an Authentic Spirit-Filled Life:

Acknowledgments

I would like to thank the following for walking with me on this road to enlightened living which resulted in the creation of this book:

To Spirit, God, and Guru- With you, all things are possible...

To my family, whom I love with all my heart. I thank you for your patience, support, and understanding through this transformational year.

To Tracy McCasey, my editor, writing coach, cheerleader, and friend. This book would not have been born without your creative genius. You are a miracle worker!

To Pam Daugavietis for your friendship, motivation, creativity, and wealth of words.

To Laura Dangel-Shaw for your delightful artistic renderings and your generous heart for sharing them.

To Bonnie and Michael Zachary for friendship, creative energy, and technical support.

To Don and Sherrie Wisner for friendship, encouragement, and proof reading.

To The Dominican Center at Marywood and Cybele's of Twin Lake for providing sacred space for my writing.

I would like to add a special hug of thanks and love to all the dear friends who walked through the fire of this last year with me. I adore all of you!

I also offer gratitude and blessings for the many angels in human form who have crossed my path this year. I am a better person for having known you.

And last but not least, I thank my God-given mentors, kind, loving, and generous individuals whose wise words continue to guide me towards the awakened life:

> Sue Patton Thoele
> Daphne Rose Kingma and
> Kenny and Julia Loggins

God bless you all. May your stars shine forever.......

About the Artist

With a needle-sized pen, the smallest of brushes, and a drop or two of watercolor pain, artist Laura Dangel-Shaw creates a whimsical world of wonder, imagination, and just plain fun, delighting fans across the country.

"I have loved doing little tiny drawings since I was young. Taking a simple design and bringing it to life by embellishing it with detail has always captivated me. My hope is that my drawings make people smile and perhaps touches something they feel in their hearts."

Laura's work includes a successful magnet art line, tiny framed originals, and greeting cards available in select retail shops since 1996. "When a good friend once said my art was like 'aromatherapy for the eyes,' I knew I had found my calling!"

Laura Dangel-Shaw can be contacted through e-mail:
DangelShawArt@aol.com

About the Author

Jan Forrest continues to be a spiritual asset to many, as her gentle, guiding presence introduces us to ways of living with serenity, purpose, and joy. Her highly requested workshops and acclaimed writings are invaluable experiences, offering a wholesome path to significant living in our day.

Jan is an educator, inspirational speaker, columnist, and the author o
Coming Home to Ourselves: A Woman's Journey to Wholeness
(Heart to Heart Press, 1999).
Her reputation as an expert in simplifying women's lives
is known throughout the U.S.
She lives with her husband and their children
along the peaceful shores of Lake Michigan.

For further information...

on Jan Forrest's inspirational workshops,
a schedule of appearances or to obtain
autographed copies of her books contact:

Heart to Heart Press
P.O.Box 215, West Olive, MI 49460
1-800-341-5541
hearttoheart@novagate.com